My First ACROSTIC
ANIMAL ADVENTURES

Amazing Rhymes

Edited By Debbie Killingworth

First published in Great Britain in 2020 by:
🟦 Young**Writers**®
— Est. 1991 —

Young Writers
Remus House
Coltsfoot Drive
Peterborough
PE2 9BF
Telephone: 01733 890066
Website: www.youngwriters.co.uk

All Rights Reserved
Book Design by Ashley Janson
© Copyright Contributors 2020
Softback ISBN 978-1-83928-982-8

Printed and bound in the UK by BookPrintingUK
Website: www.bookprintinguk.com
YB0445Y

Dear Reader,

Welcome to a fun-filled book of acrostic poems!

Here at Young Writers, we are delighted to introduce our new poetry competition for KS1 pupils, *My First Acrostic: Animal Adventures*. Acrostic poems are an enjoyable way to introduce pupils to the world of poetry and allow the young writer to open their imagination to a range of topics of their choice. The colourful and engaging entry forms allowed even the youngest (or most reluctant) of pupils to create a poem using the acrostic technique and with that, encouraged them to include other literary techniques such as similes and description. Here at Young Writers we are passionate about introducing the love and art of creative writing to the next generation and we love being a part of their journey.

From the jungle to the ocean, pets to mythical monsters, these pupils take you on a journey through the animal kingdom and showcase their budding creativity along the way. So we invite you to dive into these pages and take a glimpse into these blossoming young writers' minds. We hope you will relish these roarsome poems as much as we have.

contents

All Saints Benhilton CE Primary School, Sutton

Shania Deborah (7)	1
Simeon Babigumira (6)	2
Hannah Bentley (6)	3
Anneliese Pink (6)	4
Inara Uddin (5)	5
Chace Pienaar (5)	6
Emrys Hopping (7)	7
Harley Hammond (5)	8
Shane Navaratnarajah (7)	9
Caleb Ariyanayagam (5)	10
James Whittingham-Jones (7)	11

Arngask Primary School, Glenfarg

Thomas Nicholls (6)	12
Oliver Lochtie (5)	13
Monty Burgess (6)	14
Robert Nicholls (6)	15
Ruby McLean (6)	16

Cestria Primary School, Church Chare

Charlotte Hastie (6)	17
Lily Paige Richardson (6)	18
Libby Best (6)	19
Libby Simpson (6)	20
Marcy Wright (7)	21
Penny McCann (6)	22
Evie Nelson (7)	23
Nathan Heselwood (7)	24
Alice Agavriloae (7)	25
Isabel Kirkwood (7)	26

Brody Coffer (7)	27
Lacey-Mai Cowen (6)	28
Cecille Masters (6)	29
Ellis Green (7)	30
Ruby Parker (6)	31

Cranford Primary School, Cranford

Sonia Kaur Sangha (6)	32

Gorsemoor Primary School, Heath Hayes

Tobias Wainwright (6)	33
Chloe Harford (6)	34
Aevalynn Duffy (6)	35
Ryan Cresswell (6)	36
Henry Leighton (6)	37
Sienna Griffiths (6)	38
Corey Groves (5)	39
Daphne Shepherd (5)	40
Kady Sheeran (5)	41
Skyla Owen (6)	42
Rosanna Delaney (6)	43
Oscar Thirlby (6)	44
Addison Sheppard (5)	45
Lydia Watson (6)	46
Alfie Smith (6)	47
Martha Mattox (6)	48
Leighton Hammonds (6)	49
Melissa Lloyd (6)	50
Lily Miles (5)	51
Archie Hough (6)	52
Jack Sampson (5)	53
Felicity Yates (5)	54

Ollie Lewis-Wright (5)	55
Stanley Spicer (5)	56
Mason Carter (5)	57
Edie Aldworth (5)	58
Jake May (5)	59
Alexis Day (6)	60
Lucas Bagley (6)	61
Max Gallear (5)	62
Georgia Green (6)	63
Brandon Kite (6)	64
Harry Smith (6)	65
Joshua Stanton (5)	66
Tilly Haden (6)	67
Elliott Aldworth (5)	68
Alex Whitehouse (5)	69
Ellis Parker (6)	70
Emily Forrester (5)	71
Ivy Lawless (5), Jacob & Reid	72
Archie Wilkes (5)	73
Evie Aston (5)	74
Carter Bannister (5)	75

Gosbecks Primary School, Shrub End

Harrison Shortland (5)	76
Violet Harris (6)	77

Pardes House Primary School, Finchley

Moishe W (5)	78
Avi Kornbluth (6)	79
Chezki Cohen (7)	80
Ariel W (7)	81
Ariel Feiner (7)	82
Tuvia Deutsch (6)	83

Sledmere Primary School, Dudley

Darcie Wilkinson (5)	84
Malacai Davies (6)	85
Halimah Idrees (6)	86
Joey Griffiths (5)	87

St Joseph's Primary School, Crossgar

Maria Rooney (7)	88
Faye Cullen (6)	89
Rene McKinley (6)	90
Maya Mullan (6)	91
Maya Brennan (6)	92
Kyle Patterson (6)	93
Holly Miskelly (6)	94
Eimear McMenamin (6)	95
Aoife McLoughlin (5)	96
Ronan Irvine (5)	97
Daniel Bell (6)	98
Ronan McLaughlin (7)	99
Zac Dougan (6)	100
Caitlin McGonnell (5)	101
Katie Hamilton (5)	102
Emer Irvine (7)	103
Alfie Elliott (5)	104
Emma Hamilton (5)	105
Ryan Rowden (7)	106

Stowford School, Ivybridge

Phoebe Pearce (6)	107
Oliver Belton (6)	108
Eloise Westrope (6)	109
Amber Wavish (5)	110
Amelia Hollingsworth (5)	111
Joseph Scott (5)	112
Imogen Townshend (5)	113
Ella Poate (5)	114
Beth Bingham (6)	115

Yewstock School, Sturminster Newton

Natalie Scammell (6)	116
Charlie Ridout (6)	117
Sienna Moss (7)	118
Cruze Edwards (6)	119
Ben O'Loughlin (6)	120

The Poems

Unicorns

U nicorns flying peacefully in the sky.
N ow it's time to see them fly.
I t's time you believe the magic you see.
C ome and join us to believe.
O h come see the unicorns all night long, but now it's time to say goodnight.
R ight in the city unicorns fly, searching for diamonds in the sky.
N ow in the city unicorns are dreaming about wonderful things they have seen.

Shania Deborah (7)
All Saints Benhilton CE Primary School, Sutton

King Hippo

H appy, huge and bouncy.
I nside the water.
P laying freely.
P ast the reeds I splash.
O n a sunny day.
P owerful moves, *whoosh, whoosh!*
O ver and over.
T urning from side to side.
A nimals getting out of my way.
M ove, move, here I come.
U nmatched.
S trong and mighty.

Simeon Babigumira (6)
All Saints Benhilton CE Primary School, Sutton

Flamingo Dance

F luffy little creatures.
L azy creatures too.
A wesome, cool and wonderful.
M ystical, doobeedoo!
I magine all the tricks they'd get up to.
N obody would ever see.
G reat mischief-makers.
O h... how wonderful they are.

Hannah Bentley (6)
All Saints Benhilton CE Primary School, Sutton

A Wonderful Dream

U nbelievable dream.
N ever want it to stop.
I ts magical powers fill the air.
C urly, fluffy tails waving at me.
O ver the rainbow unicorns fly.
R iding fast, flapping their colourful wings.
N ever want to wake up.

Anneliese Pink (6)
All Saints Benhilton CE Primary School, Sutton

Penguin Land

P layful with its friends.
E nergetic in the water.
N ormally waddles on the land.
G entle with its eggs.
U nited together.
I n the white snow.
N eat black and white fur.

Inara Uddin (5)
All Saints Benhilton CE Primary School, Sutton

Cheetahs

C hasing animals.
H ot and tired.
E very day in the sun.
E legant creatures.
T errific and bold.
A lways eating.
H unting prey.
S potty cheetahs here to stay.

Chace Pienaar (5)
All Saints Benhilton CE Primary School, Sutton

Jump Jump Rabbit

R abbits jumping up and down
A gile and cute
B ouncing, bouncing all around
B urrowing into the ground
I nquisitive and fluffy
T ucking into carrots that are nice and yummy

Emrys Hopping (7)
All Saints Benhilton CE Primary School, Sutton

Unicorns

U nicorns are magical.
N aturally fly free.
I ncredibly rare.
C hase rainbows.
O ver mountains.
R un fast.
N ever seen.
S parkle brightly.

Harley Hammond (5)
All Saints Benhilton CE Primary School, Sutton

Dragons Rule

D ragons, dragons
R acing through the air
A nd swooping through the air
G racefully.
O h, what will it be like to have a
N ice baby dragon?

Shane Navaratnarajah (7)
All Saints Benhilton CE Primary School, Sutton

Rhino

R hinos are big.
H orns are for charging.
I ndestructible.
N oses are for smelling.
O ver in Africa you will find lots and lots of rhinos.

Caleb Ariyanayagam (5)
All Saints Benhilton CE Primary School, Sutton

Lion

L ife on land.
I ncredible.
O ver and above king of the plains.
N ot nice but mean.

James Whittingham-Jones (7)
All Saints Benhilton CE Primary School, Sutton

Leopard

L eopard is eating meat.
E verything is different for leopards.
O utside the leopard was eating.
P ouncing leopard.
A frica was melting the leopards.
R acing other leopards.
D ifferent day.

Thomas Nicholls (6)
Arngask Primary School, Glenfarg

I Like Penguins

P enguins swim.
E very day they swim.
N ever go swimming with nets.
G et an ice block.
U p went the penguin.
I t was cool.
N ice penguins.

Oliver Lochtie (5)
Arngask Primary School, Glenfarg

The Chicks

C hicks come from eggs.
H ow do chicks come from eggs?
I t was small.
C ould have a chick.
K ind chickens lay eggs.

Monty Burgess (6)
Arngask Primary School, Glenfarg

Fighting Tigers

T ough tigers.
I t is good to see them.
G reat fighters.
E xciting for humans to see them.
R acing together.

Robert Nicholls (6)
Arngask Primary School, Glenfarg

About The Dog

D og did jump.
O n the dog there was a collar.
G ood dog for eating your treat.

Ruby McLean (6)
Arngask Primary School, Glenfarg

Unicorns

U nicorns.
N ever fall out with me.
I nspirational.
C lassic.
O range, purple and pink.
R ainbow hair.
N ever die.
S parkle.

Charlotte Hastie (6)
Cestria Primary School, Church Chare

Monkey

M ysterious.
O ne cheeky monkey.
N ormally snatching bananas.
K ind of silly.
E very day they eat bananas.
Y es they do.

Lily Paige Richardson (6)
Cestria Primary School, Church Chare

Jellyfish

J umpy.
E xcited.
L umpy.
L oopy.
Y ellow.
F riendly.
I ncredible.
S quishy.
H iding.

Libby Best (6)
Cestria Primary School, Church Chare

Ladybug

L ittle.
A mazing.
D elightful.
Y ellow-bellied.
B rilliant at flying.
U nique.
G orgeous.

Libby Simpson (6)
Cestria Primary School, Church Chare

Leopard

L eapy.
E pic.
O ddly cute.
P opular.
A mazing.
R eally fast.
D istracting.

Marcy Wright (7)
Cestria Primary School, Church Chare

Shark

S wimming very slowly.
H unting for fish.
A mazing animals.
R eally hungry.
K ing of the ocean.

Penny McCann (6)
Cestria Primary School, Church Chare

Tiger

T errifying animal.
I nteresting animal.
G reat animal.
E xciting animal.
R oaring animal.

Evie Nelson (7)
Cestria Primary School, Church Chare

Snake

S caly.
N o friends.
A lways ready for its prey.
K illing.
E ating.

Nathan Heselwood (7)
Cestria Primary School, Church Chare

Cats

C laws for scratching.
A lways asleep.
T ake to the vet.
S oft to touch.

Alice Agavriloae (7)
Cestria Primary School, Church Chare

Deer

D efend all the animals.
E at grass.
E xcellent animal.
R uns very fast.

Isabel Kirkwood (7)
Cestria Primary School, Church Chare

Pandas

P andas
A re
N ice
D ainty
A nd shy.

Brody Coffer (7)
Cestria Primary School, Church Chare

Bird

B eautiful.
I ntelligent.
R ide.
D ope!

Lacey-Mai Cowen (6)
Cestria Primary School, Church Chare

Dog

D ig holes.
O ne of the family.
G ood and lovely.

Cecille Masters (6)
Cestria Primary School, Church Chare

Dog

D ark-coloured fur.
O ne of my friends.
G enius.

Ellis Green (7)
Cestria Primary School, Church Chare

Fox

F luffy tail.
O rdinary.
X -ray vision.

Ruby Parker (6)
Cestria Primary School, Church Chare

Dog

H aving the best day ever.
A lways outside no matter the weather.
R unning and jumping in the rain.
V room! Vroom! Faster than a train.
E very day he has fun.
Y ellow, soft and bright like the sun.

Sonia Kaur Sangha (6)
Cranford Primary School, Cranford

Elephant

E lephants eat plants.
L ives in the jungle.
E lephants have long powerful trunks.
P roudly walking.
H appy and kind.
A big family.
N aturally knobbly grey knees.
T runks to drink with.

Tobias Wainwright (6)
Gorsemoor Primary School, Heath Hayes

Monkeys

M onkeys chomp yellow bananas.
O utside in the jungle they swing about.
N ever bring food to the safari.
K eeping each other clean.
E ach day they scratch.
Y ou can hear them screech.

Chloe Harford (6)
Gorsemoor Primary School, Heath Hayes

Monkey

M onkeys eat yellow bananas.
O utside they swing on trees.
N obody feed monkeys.
K eeping warm.
E very day they climb trees.
Y ou can hear them say 'ooh ahh ahh'.

Aevalynn Duffy (6)
Gorsemoor Primary School, Heath Hayes

Monkey

M onkeys are cheeky and naughty.
O ut in the jungle they swing about.
N obody feeds them in the wild.
K eeping clean.
E ating bananas.
Y ou can hear them howl.

Ryan Cresswell (6)
Gorsemoor Primary School, Heath Hayes

Monkey

M onkeys are cheeky.
O utside they steal bananas.
N ever stop being naughty.
K icking the trees.
E veryone gets to swing.
Y ou are so silly.

Henry Leighton (6)
Gorsemoor Primary School, Heath Hayes

Lion

L arge claws, giant paws.
I n the noisy zoo as the lion roars.
O range, glossy mane is bigger than you.
N ever ever go too close or he'll gobble you up.

Sienna Griffiths (6)
Gorsemoor Primary School, Heath Hayes

Giraffe

G old and brown spots.
I n the jungle.
R eally long legs.
A long neck.
F riendly giants.
F unny ears.
E ating leaves.

Corey Groves (5)
Gorsemoor Primary School, Heath Hayes

Monkey

M onkeys are cheeky.
O n the safari.
N o feeding them.
K issing bananas.
E very day they keep clean.
Y ou can hear them howl.

Daphne Shepherd (5)
Gorsemoor Primary School, Heath Hayes

Lion

L ions eat meat a lot.
I n the zoo lions like running.
O n the grass they like sleeping.
N aughty lions like playing games with the other lions.

Kady Sheeran (5)
Gorsemoor Primary School, Heath Hayes

Parrot

P arrots are rainbow-coloured.
A parrot can fly.
R eally bright feathers.
R ainforest.
O n the branches.
T iny feet.

Skyla Owen (6)
Gorsemoor Primary School, Heath Hayes

Hippo

H ippos are grey.
I n the water all day.
P laying with my friends.
P ushing your friends in the mud.
O utside they sleep.

Rosanna Delaney (6)
Gorsemoor Primary School, Heath Hayes

Hippo

H ippos are grey.
I n the mud they play.
P laying with friends.
P ushing each other.
O n the riverbank they play.

Oscar Thirlby (6)
Gorsemoor Primary School, Heath Hayes

Tiger

T igers have sharp claws.
I n the jungle they live.
G reat big teeth.
E ating their prey.
R acing in the jungle.

Addison Sheppard (5)
Gorsemoor Primary School, Heath Hayes

Lion

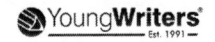

L ions are strong and powerful.
I t has sharp claws and sharp teeth.
O n the rock it's eating.
N obody touches him.

Lydia Watson (6)
Gorsemoor Primary School, Heath Hayes

Tiger

T igers are orange like the sun.
I n Africa they hunt.
G reat beast.
E xtremely fast.
R oaming for prey.

Alfie Smith (6)
Gorsemoor Primary School, Heath Hayes

Lion

L ion has a cave.
I t has sharp teeth and claws.
O n the loose.
N ever get close to a lion or it will growl at you.

Martha Mattox (6)
Gorsemoor Primary School, Heath Hayes

Tiger

T igers are fierce.
I n the jungle they hunt.
G rowling loudly.
E ating their prey.
R acing around.

Leighton Hammonds (6)
Gorsemoor Primary School, Heath Hayes

Panda

P andas are black and white.
A furry tummy.
N ibbles on bamboo.
D ark black eyes.
A wet nose.

Melissa Lloyd (6)
Gorsemoor Primary School, Heath Hayes

Snake

S nakes are long.
N ever have I seen one.
A snake slithers.
K eep them warm.
E xtremely scary.

Lily Miles (5)
Gorsemoor Primary School, Heath Hayes

Snake

S lithering snake.
N o bones.
A lways hissing.
K eep wriggling.
E veryone's excited.

Archie Hough (6)
Gorsemoor Primary School, Heath Hayes

Tigers

T igers are stripy.
I n the jungle.
G rowling.
E ating their prey.
R unning very fast.

Jack Sampson (5)
Gorsemoor Primary School, Heath Hayes

Lion

L ion on the loose.
I n Gorsemoor he roared.
O n his face is a wet nose.
N ow the school is safe.

Felicity Yates (5)
Gorsemoor Primary School, Heath Hayes

Lion

L ion on the loose
I n Gorsemoor Primary School.
O utside he pounced.
N ow the school is safe.

Ollie Lewis-Wright (5)
Gorsemoor Primary School, Heath Hayes

Lion

L ions are fluffy.
I n the jungle.
O n his face are whiskers.
N ibbles with his sharp teeth.

Stanley Spicer (5)
Gorsemoor Primary School, Heath Hayes

Lion

L arge paws and big teeth.
I n the zoo there are lions.
O n the trees.
N ever go too close.

Mason Carter (5)
Gorsemoor Primary School, Heath Hayes

Lion

L ion has a furry mane.
I n the jungle.
O n his body is soft fur.
N ow the school is safe.

Edie Aldworth (5)
Gorsemoor Primary School, Heath Hayes

Lion

L ions have a glossy mane.
I n the quiet zoo.
O range furry body.
N ever go too close.

Jake May (5)
Gorsemoor Primary School, Heath Hayes

Lion

L ions have sharp teeth.
I n the noisy zoo.
O n the tree.
N ever creep up on a lion.

Alexis Day (6)
Gorsemoor Primary School, Heath Hayes

Lion

L ions have sharp teeth.
I 'm ready to eat.
O n the trees.
N ever go too close.

Lucas Bagley (6)
Gorsemoor Primary School, Heath Hayes

Lion

L ions have sharp teeth.
I ncredible big claws.
O utside he roared.
N aughty lion.

Max Gallear (5)
Gorsemoor Primary School, Heath Hayes

Lion

L ion on the loose?
I ncredible roars.
O utside he pounces.
N ever get too close!

Georgia Green (6)
Gorsemoor Primary School, Heath Hayes

Lion

L arge, glossy mane.
I n the noisy zoo.
O range, furry body.
N ever go too close.

Brandon Kite (6)
Gorsemoor Primary School, Heath Hayes

Lion

L arge, big jaws.
I 'm ready to eat meat.
O range body.
N ice furry back.

Harry Smith (6)
Gorsemoor Primary School, Heath Hayes

Lion

L ions eat a lot.
I n the noisy zoo.
O range glossy mane.
N oisily sleep.

Joshua Stanton (5)
Gorsemoor Primary School, Heath Hayes

Lion

L ion roars.
I ncredible claws.
O utside they play.
N ice friendly lion.

Tilly Haden (6)
Gorsemoor Primary School, Heath Hayes

Lion

L ions have soft fur.
I ncredible teeth.
O pen jaws.
N ot too friendly.

Elliott Aldworth (5)
Gorsemoor Primary School, Heath Hayes

Lion

L ion on the loose.
I n my school.
O utside he crept.
N ow he has gone.

Alex Whitehouse (5)
Gorsemoor Primary School, Heath Hayes

Lion

L arge fluffy mane.
I t's hungry.
O n a hunt.
N ever go near it.

Ellis Parker (6)
Gorsemoor Primary School, Heath Hayes

Lion

L ions have sharp teeth.
I n a loud zoo.
O n a stone.
N aughty lion.

Emily Forrester (5)
Gorsemoor Primary School, Heath Hayes

Lion

L arge lion.
I n the jungle.
O n the rocks.
N asty, sharp teeth.

Ivy Lawless (5), Jacob & Reid
Gorsemoor Primary School, Heath Hayes

Lion

L arge lion
I n the jungle.
O range mane.
N asty sharp teeth.

Archie Wilkes (5)
Gorsemoor Primary School, Heath Hayes

Lion

L ost lion
I n the cave.
O range, glossy mane.
N oisy paws.

Evie Aston (5)
Gorsemoor Primary School, Heath Hayes

Lion

L arge lion
I s on the hunt.
O n the loose.
N aughty lion.

Carter Bannister (5)
Gorsemoor Primary School, Heath Hayes

Elephant

E lephants are mammals.
L arge yet gentle.
E lephants are beautiful.
P lants, grass and fruit are their favourite food.
H appiest when they have a swim.
A ll part of a large family.
N o elephant ever forgets.
T hat's why I love them so.

Harrison Shortland (5)
Gosbecks Primary School, Shrub End

Giraffe

G igantic necks.
I ncredibly tall.
R eally long legs.
A beautiful animal.
F ound munching leaves.
F ound on the savannah.
E veryone loves giraffes.

Violet Harris (6)
Gosbecks Primary School, Shrub End

Dinosaur

D angerous naughty dinosaur, you bit my friend.
I know you're eating all my friends and cousins.
N aughty dinosaur, you're so naughty and I hate you.
O ldest animal in the world.
S houting loud all the time.
A n extinct animal.
U gly, stinky dinosaur, I hate you.
R eally, there are no more in the wild.

Moishe W (5)
Pardes House Primary School, Finchley

Lions

L ions like to lie on the floor.
I ncluding mummy lions.
O nly daddy lions like to lie on the tree.
N aughty ones don't get a bone for lunch.
S ensible lions do have a bone for lunch.

Avi Kornbluth (6)
Pardes House Primary School, Finchley

Lion

L oves to chase other animals and leaps onto them.
I t always runs into battle.
O h, it is scary!
N ever runs away from battles and its golden mane glows.

Chezki Cohen (7)
Pardes House Primary School, Finchley

Lion

L oves eating people.
I don't like lions.
O h I think he is hungry.
N o, maybe he isn't!

Ariel W (7)
Pardes House Primary School, Finchley

Cat

C ute and cuddly.
A nd drink milk.
T hey like to purr.

Ariel Feiner (7)
Pardes House Primary School, Finchley

Owl

O dd.
W ild.
L oud at night.

Tuvia Deutsch (6)
Pardes House Primary School, Finchley

Hedgehog Adventure

H appiness you will see.
E very time you look at me.
D arkness is when I come out to play.
G reen grass is where I hide away.
E very time I see a light I
H ide away as I feel a fright.
O ver your garden I will run,
G etting home before the sun.

Darcie Wilkinson (5)
Sledmere Primary School, Dudley

Amazing Adventures

B utterfly adventures.
U nder the bridge.
T all trees all around.
T o the forest.
E verything is green.
R ound the trees and bushes.
F lying through the sky.
L anding on a red rose.
Y ippee! She's finished the trail.

Malacai Davies (6)
Sledmere Primary School, Dudley

Gabriella The Giraffe

G iant giraffe grabbing leaves.
I ntelligently it walks along the ground.
R igid and long it stares at the sky.
A lways hungry.
F riendly to everyone it meets.
F abulous patchwork on its neck.
E nergetic.

Halimah Idrees (6)
Sledmere Primary School, Dudley

Penguins

P enguins have a beak.
E very penguin likes to swim.
N ests made of stone.
G ather round ice.
U nder the water.
I ce is their home.
N ice and fluffy.

Joey Griffiths (5)
Sledmere Primary School, Dudley

Unicorn

U p in the clouds soaring high.
N ever ever seen before.
I saw the most magical sight.
C razy and colourful.
O ver the sky sparkling bright.
R ainbow horn and rainbow tail.
N eighing like a pony for all to hear.

Maria Rooney (7)
St Joseph's Primary School, Crossgar

Unicorn Poem

U nicorns are magical horses.
N ice and pretty unicorns.
I love unicorns.
C urly manes and tails are rainbow-coloured.
O ur unicorns smell of lemon.
R ainbow is her name.
N obody is allowed to touch unicorns.

Faye Cullen (6)
St Joseph's Primary School, Crossgar

Kitten

K itten, kitten, quite so cute.
I love to play with you so much.
T ime with you is so much fun.
T ickling you on your tum.
E ars that twitch and whiskers that itch.
N ose that sparkles in the night sky.

Rene McKinley (6)
St Joseph's Primary School, Crossgar

Unicorn Dreams

U nicorns are magical.
N icest animal ever.
I magine it can fly.
C olourful and sparkly.
O r white and purple tail.
R ainbows appear when they are near.
N ow I dream of my own.

Maya Mullan (6)
St Joseph's Primary School, Crossgar

The Dolphin

D olphins like to play.
O n the water and
L ove splashing people.
P laying with children.
H iding underwater.
I n the ocean.
N ot too near the shore.

Maya Brennan (6)
St Joseph's Primary School, Crossgar

Dinosaur

D inosaur, dinosaur
I n the museum.
N o need to be scared.
O nly remains.
S o have a look
A nd explore
U ntil you hear a dinosaur
R oar!

Kyle Patterson (6)
St Joseph's Primary School, Crossgar

Dolphin

D eep in the ocean.
O ut they jump.
L eaping in the air.
P laying with their friends.
H ungry for fish.
I n they splash.
N ever stop smiling.

Holly Miskelly (6)
St Joseph's Primary School, Crossgar

Unicorn

U nicorns are so sparkly.
N ose so bright.
I n the sky.
C an you see it?
O ver the rainbow.
R acing on.
N ow it has disappeared.

Eimear McMenamin (6)
St Joseph's Primary School, Crossgar

Magic

M y unicorn is called Twinkle Toes
A nd she is pretty.
G alloping through the fields
I n summer with her
C olourful hair.

Aoife McLoughlin (5)
St Joseph's Primary School, Crossgar

Hippo

H ippos are huge.
I love their teeth.
P uddles are where they play.
P ooing is what they do.
O ften they go into water.

Ronan Irvine (5)
St Joseph's Primary School, Crossgar

Turtle

T ommy the turtle.
U p the hill.
R eally slow.
T o the top.
L et's have a picnic.
E veryone had fun.

Daniel Bell (6)
St Joseph's Primary School, Crossgar

Dino Dinner

D o not
I nterrupt
N asty,
O ld,
S harp-toothed,
A ngry,
U nfed
R eptiles.

Ronan McLaughlin (7)
St Joseph's Primary School, Crossgar

Dog

D ogs can be different sizes and colours.
O ur cousin has a small terrier.
G od always loves us even when we are bad.

Zac Dougan (6)
St Joseph's Primary School, Crossgar

My Furry Friend

C ute and cuddly pet.
A lways up to mischief.
T ail wagging merrily.
S uch a special friend to me.

Caitlin McGonnell (5)
St Joseph's Primary School, Crossgar

Naughty Dog

D igging up the garden.
O n the hunt for a bone.
G etting into trouble all on their own.

Katie Hamilton (5)
St Joseph's Primary School, Crossgar

Dog

D ogs are stinky.
O ften they bark.
G oing for walks is what they love to do.

Emer Irvine (7)
St Joseph's Primary School, Crossgar

Dog

D ogs love to bark.
O ur dog has fun.
G od loves my dog, Samson.

Alfie Elliott (5)
St Joseph's Primary School, Crossgar

Lazy Cat

C ute and funny.
A lways looking to nap.
T he little lazy cat.

Emma Hamilton (5)
St Joseph's Primary School, Crossgar

A Man's Best Friend

D ogs are always
O ver-excited when they
G reet their owners.

Ryan Rowden (7)
St Joseph's Primary School, Crossgar

Sleep Tight, Honey

H oney the hedgehog arrived in my garden.
E ating worms and slugs and some
D og food that I put out.
G reedy Honey ate it all!
E very night she did the same until
H ibernation time came.
O f course she will sleep all winter long.
G osh, how I miss her now she has gone!

Phoebe Pearce (6)
Stowford School, Ivybridge

Stegosaurus

S piky.
T ail to swish.
E ats plants.
G iant.
O ver-sized.
S mall brain.
A rmour-plated back.
U nusual.
R oofed lizard.
U nreal.
S tegosaurus.

Oliver Belton (6)
Stowford School, Ivybridge

Elephant Poem

E ars that hear.
L ong swingy trunk.
E yes like pools of terrible fire.
P ulling down trees.
H eavy and muddy.
A happy animal.
N oisy family.
T ail that goes swish swish!

Eloise Westrope (6)
Stowford School, Ivybridge

Una The Unicorn

U na the unicorn is yellow.
N ice she is in and out.
I think she is the most beautiful.
C olourful, sparkly hair.
O h up high she flies.
R osy cheeks glowing.
N odding with delight.

Amber Wavish (5)
Stowford School, Ivybridge

A Giraffe

G iant, long neck.
I cky black tongue.
R eaching the tallest trees.
A lmost touching the clouds.
F amily in a herd.
F ound wild in Africa.
E ating lots of leaves.

Amelia Hollingsworth (5)
Stowford School, Ivybridge

Koala

K oalas eat eucalyptus.
O n tall trees.
A nd their fur is soft.
L ive in Australia.
A nd they are my favourite animal.

Joseph Scott (5)
Stowford School, Ivybridge

Unicorn Magic

U nicorns
N ever
I magine
C ats
O n
R ivers,
N o
S iree!

Imogen Townshend (5)
Stowford School, Ivybridge

Horse

H erd.
O n your saddle.
R iding.
S pirit.
E nergy.

Ella Poate (5)
Stowford School, Ivybridge

Cats

C urled up
A sleep on
T he
S ofa.

Beth Bingham (6)
Stowford School, Ivybridge

Rainbow Unicorn

U nicorns are good.
N ice.
I like unicorns.
C ute.
O h look.
R unning with friends.
N ow they sleep.

Natalie Scammell (6)
Yewstock School, Sturminster Newton

Godzilla King Monster

D ragons are black.
R oar!
A re happy.
G odzilla.
O h no!
N aughty dragon.

Charlie Ridout (6)
Yewstock School, Sturminster Newton

Olivia

P uppies eat food
U nder the table.
P layful puppy.
P lays.
Y ellow lead.

Sienna Moss (7)
Yewstock School, Sturminster Newton

Roar!

T eeth are big.
-
R oar is loud.
E ats lots.
e **X** tra long.

Cruze Edwards (6)
Yewstock School, Sturminster Newton

Puppy

D ogs are small.
O h no!
G ood dog.

Ben O'Loughlin (6)
Yewstock School, Sturminster Newton

Young Writers Information

We hope you have enjoyed reading this book – and that you will continue to in the coming years.

If you're a young writer who enjoys reading and creative writing, or the parent of an enthusiastic poet or story writer, do visit our website **www.youngwriters.co.uk**. Here you will find free competitions, workshops and games, as well as recommended reads, a poetry glossary and our blog. There's lots to keep budding writers motivated to write!

If you would like to order further copies of this book, or any of our other titles, then please give us a call or order via your online account.

Young Writers
Remus House
Coltsfoot Drive
Peterborough
PE2 9BF
(01733) 890066
info@youngwriters.co.uk

Join in the conversation!
Tips, news, giveaways and much more!

YoungWritersUK   @YoungWritersCW